*GREATER T
AVAILABLE IN EBOOK AND AUDIOBOOK.

Greater Than a Tourist Book Series Reviews from Readers

I think the series is wonderful and beneficial for tourists to get information before visiting the city.
-Seckin Zumbul, Izmir Turkey

I am a world traveler who has read many trip guides but this one really made a difference for me. I would call it a heartfelt creation of a local guide expert instead of just a guide.
-Susy, Isla Holbox, Mexico

New to the area like me, this is a must have!
 -Joe, Bloomington, USA

This is a good series that gets down to it when looking for things to do at your destination without having to read a novel for just a few ideas.
-Rachel, Monterey, USA

Good information to have to plan my trip to this destination.

-Pennie Farrell, Mexico

Great ideas for a port day.

-Mary Martin USA

Aptly titled, you won't just be a tourist after reading this book. You'll be greater than a tourist!

-Alan Warner, Grand Rapids, USA

Even though I only have three days to spend in San Miguel in an upcoming visit, I will use the author's suggestions to guide some of my time there. An easy read - with chapters named to guide me in directions I want to go.

 -Robert Catapano, USA

Great insights from a local perspective! Useful information and a very good value!

 -Sarah, USA

This series provides an in-depth experience through the eyes of a local. Reading these series will help you to travel the city in with confidence and it'll make your journey a unique one.

-Andrew Teoh, Ipoh, Malaysia

>TOURIST

GREATER THAN A TOURIST- ICELAND

50 Travel Tips from a Local

Angie Diamantopoulou

Greater Than a Tourist-Iceland Copyright © 2019 by CZYK Publishing LLC. All Rights Reserved.

All rights reserved. No part of this book may be reproduced in any form or by any electronic or mechanical means including information storage and retrieval systems, without permission in writing from the author. The only exception is by a reviewer, who may quote short excerpts in a review.

The statements in this book are of the authors and may not be the views of CZYK Publishing or Greater Than a Tourist.

Cover designed by: Ivana Stamenkovic
Cover Image: https://pixabay.com/photos/iceland-landscape-sey%C3%B0isfj%C3%B6r%C3%B0ur-3516723/

CZYK Publishing Since 2011.

Greater Than a Tourist

Lock Haven, PA
All rights reserved.

ISBN: 9781706210344

>TOURIST

50 TRAVEL TIPS FROM A LOCAL

BOOK DESCRIPTION

Are you excited about planning your next trip? Do you want to try something new? Would you like some guidance from a local? If you answered yes to any of these questions, then this Greater Than a Tourist book is for you. x. Most travel books tell you how to travel like a tourist. Although there is nothing wrong with that, as part of the Greater Than a Tourist series, this book will give you travel tips from someone who has lived at your next travel destination.

In these pages, you will discover advice that will help you throughout your stay. This book will not tell you exact addresses or store hours but instead will give you excitement and knowledge from a local that you may not find in other smaller print travel books.

Travel like a local. Slow down, stay in one place, and get to know the people and culture. By the time you finish this book, you will be eager and prepared to travel to your next destination.

Inside this travel guide book you will find:

- Insider tips from a local.
- Packing and planning list.
- List of travel questions to ask yourself or others while traveling.
- A place to write your travel bucket list.

OUR STORY

Traveling is a passion of the Greater than a Tourist book series creator. Lisa studied abroad in college, and for their honeymoon Lisa and her husband toured Europe. During her travels to Malta, an older man tried to give her some advice based on his own experience living on the island since he was a young boy. She was not sure if she should talk to the stranger but was interested in his advice. When traveling to some places she was wary to talk to locals because she was afraid that they weren't being genuine. Through her travels, Lisa learned how much locals had to share with tourists. Lisa created the Greater Than a Tourist book series to help connect people with locals. A topic that locals are very passionate about sharing.

>TOURIST

TABLE OF CONTENTS

BOOK DESCRIPTION
OUR STORY
TABLE OF CONTENTS
DEDICATION
ABOUT THE AUTHOR
HOW TO USE THIS BOOK
FROM THE PUBLISHER
WELCOME TO
> TOURIST

Act Like A Real Icelander

1. Keep Your Car On The Road And Your Feet On The Path
2. Recycle
3. Always Carry A Water Bottle
4. A Tip About Tipping
5. ay With Your Card . . . Or Your Phone, Or Your Watch

Enjoy Reykjavik

6. Visit Reykjavik's Crown Jewel, Hallgrímskirkja
7. Admire The Architecture Of Harpa
8. See The View From Perlan
9. Visit The Pond
10. Every Day Is Christmas At The Christmas Store
11. Get A City Card

12. Tired Of Walking? Get An Electric Scooter

What To Do And What To See

13. Enjoy A Swim In Iceland's Swimming Pools
14. Relax In A Hot Spring
15. Look Into The Past On A Glacier
16. Get Drenched Under A Waterfall
17. Walk Between Two Continents

Day Trips From Reykjavik

18. Visit Snæfellsnes
19. Travel Along The South Shore
20. Visit The Golden Circle
21. Visit Reykjanes
22. Hike Up Esja
23. Hike And Soak In Reykjadalur

Getting Around

24. Rent A Car
25. Book A Tour
26. Take The Bus

Icelandic Delights

27. Eat The World's Best Hot Dog
28. Indulge In Candy (Or As We Say, Nammi)
29. Give The Dried Fish A Try
30. A Taste Fox A Day Will Make You Want To Stay
31. Taste Tradition With Lamb And Lamb Soup
32. Try The World-Famous Skyr

33. Try Brennivín . . . If You Dare

Souvenirs To Remind You Of Your Travels

34. Lopapeysa Knitted By A Grandma
35. Take A Taste Of Iceland Home With You With Some Candy
36. Indulge In Handmade Jewelry

What Festivals To Attend

37. Party Like A Local At Þjóðhátíð
38. Enjoy Music Under The Midnight Sun At Secret Solstice
39. See Underground Acts In Reykjavik's Best Venues At Iceland Airwaves
40. Try Mouthwatering Delicacies At Reykjavik Food Festival

Activities For The Whole Family

41. Go Skiing
42. Try Snowmobiling
43. Go On A Glacier Hike
44. Sightsee At The Sea
45. Try To See Some Puffins
46. Ride The World-Famous Icelandic Horse
47. Aching For Some Off-Roading? Go On An ATV Ride

What To Pack For Your Trip

48. For The Winter
49. For The Summer

50. Don't Forget Your Camera
Can't Get Enough? Here Are Some Bonus Tips
TOP REASONS TO BOOK THIS TRIP
Other Resources:
Packing and Planning Tips
Travel Questions
Travel Bucket List
NOTES

DEDICATION

This book is dedicated to Arnór, for taking the time to show me his beautiful country and making me fall in love with its landscapes.

ABOUT THE AUTHOR

Angie is an artist who has lived Reykjavik for the past three years, but is a native of Athens and has lived all over the world. Angie loves to write, read books while snacking on Icelandic candy (more on that later), and play with dogs that sadly don't belong to her.

Angie loves to travel…

>TOURIST

HOW TO USE THIS BOOK

The *Greater Than a Tourist* book series was written by someone who has lived in an area for over three months. The goal of this book is to help travelers either dream or experience different locations by providing opinions from a local. The author has made suggestions based on their own experiences. Please check before traveling to the area in case the suggested places are unavailable.

Travel Advisories: As a first step in planning any trip abroad, check the Travel Advisories for your intended destination.
https://travel.state.gov/content/travel/en/traveladvisories/traveladvisories.html

FROM THE PUBLISHER

Traveling can be one of the most important parts of a person's life. The anticipation and memories that you have are some of the best. As a publisher of the Greater Than a Tourist, as well as the popular *50 Things to Know* book series, we strive to help you learn about new places, spark your imagination, and inspire you. Wherever you are and whatever you do I wish you safe, fun, and inspiring travel.

Lisa Rusczyk Ed. D.
CZYK Publishing

>TOURIST

WELCOME TO
> TOURIST

>TOURIST

"The impulse to travel is one of the hopeful symptoms of life."

— Agnes Repplier

There is this belief, at the back of my mind, that Iceland exists in a time paradox. A land so ancient, the glimpses of past millennia cracking through the modern hubbub of Reykjavik in the form of lava fields covered in moss and glacial ice crackling as it breaks, ever-changing. The same, but different. A land where three years can seem like an eternity or a blink of an eye, where you are a local within a few hours or a few decades.

This is what I want for you; to become a local when you step foot outside the Keflavik International Airport, and feel right at home in this strange, beautiful, eternal place, after reading my top tips and do's and don'ts of visiting Iceland.

>TOURIST

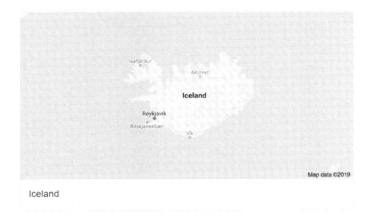

Iceland

Reykjavik Iceland Climate

	High	Low
January	37	27
February	38	28
March	39	29
April	43	33
May	49	39
June	54	44
July	57	48
August	56	47
September	51	42
October	45	36
November	39	31
December	37	28

GreaterThanaTourist.com

Temperatures are in Fahrenheit degrees.
Source: NOAA

\>TOURIST

ACT LIKE A REAL ICELANDER

1. KEEP YOUR CAR ON THE ROAD AND YOUR FEET ON THE PATH

Ask any Icelandic person –or any person who has lived in Iceland for long enough –and they will tell you that their biggest pet peeve is seeing a tourist happily, recklessly off-roading. Iceland might seem like the perfect place to rent a 4x4 and drive over lava fields and black sand beaches, but by doing so, you destroy the nature that is so important to this country.

Those rolling lava fields covered in soft, cloud-like moss are Iceland's most fragile treasure. If you drive or even step on the moss, it will take decades for it to recover and regrow, as the moss only grows a few tenths of an inch annually!

So, be considerate and help preserve the breathtaking Icelandic nature by sticking to the designated roads and paths. Besides, walking on a lava field is very dangerous, as there are several hidden holes, where the ground can, quite literally, swallow you whole. Therefore, enjoy the lava fields from a sensible distance!

2. RECYCLE

The mantra of Icelandic people? Reuse, recycle, recycle, and recycle. Everything in Iceland has a designated bin, from paper and plastic to even clothes!

You will most likely end up with a substantial amount of paper and plastic during your trip, whether it be from snack wrappers or brochures and leaflets. Make sure that you recycle everything you can! It's very easy. Every place that has a trash can also has recycling bins, so please take the extra time to throw your papers and plastic there.

3. ALWAYS CARRY A WATER BOTTLE

There are many countries around the world where you would be better off buying bottled water.

Iceland is not one of them. The most popular kind of water in Iceland is called kranavatn, and –if you haven't already guessed it –it's tap water! Iceland has some of the cleanest water in the world, as the water that reaches your tap has been filtered for 40 years through lava, which draws out every impurity. Turn your tap to cold and you will have delicious, ice-cold water in your water bottle within seconds!

Found yourself at a gas station or restaurant without water in your bottle? Feel free to ask them to refill it for you! Also feel free to fill your water bottle with water from rivers and waterfalls! Just make sure that the water looks clear, and that the area doesn't have too much foot traffic.

4. A TIP ABOUT TIPPING

If you've worked a service job, you know that tipping is always greatly appreciated. However, unlike in other countries, in Iceland you are not expected to tip. The prices at most restaurants and coffee shops are already outrageous!

If you're worried about your servers being underpaid, then I can assure you that everyone in Iceland is paid fair wages. That being said, if you feel like you received excellent service and you want to brighten your server's day, then leaving a tip will be greatly appreciated! If you're on a tight budget, though – Iceland is already expensive as it is –don't feel bad about not leaving a tip.

5. PAY WITH YOUR CARD... OR YOUR PHONE, OR YOUR WATCH

There are very few places in Iceland that don't accept credit cards or Apple Pay, and you most likely won't be visiting those places anyway. You don't have to carry cash with you, unless your bank charges you expensive fees every time you purchase something abroad.

If you would like to have cash, many places in Reykjavik accept euros and dollars. However, there are also places that don't, both in Reykjavik and mainly in other towns around Iceland. Your best bet is to carry some Icelandic crowns with you, since even if you pay with another currency, you will be given crowns as change.

>TOURIST

ENJOY REYKJAVIK

6. VISIT REYKJAVIK'S CROWN JEWEL, HALLGRÍMSKIRKJA

Reykjavik is renowned for many things; its colorful side streets, the weather that seems to have a mind of its own, the abundance of boutiques. The most famous thing in Reykjavik, though, is Hallgrímskirkja.

Hallgrímskirkja is a church located right in the heart of the capital. It towers over downtown Reykjavik, at an impressive height of approximately 244 feet! It's no wonder, then, that the church has one of the most impressive views of Reykjavik that you can find!

Hallgrímskirkja is named after Hallgrímur Pétursson, a poet and clergyman who wrote a collection of religious poems called The Passion Hymns. It took a whopping 41 years to build and was completed in 1986.

So, why should you visit Hallgrímskirkja? Well, apart from the magnificent view of Reykjavik, the building itself is a marvel of architecture. It is said that the exterior, which resembles basalt columns that are found virtually everywhere in Iceland, was inspired by the shape of a mountain range in the north of the country. Look at its distinctive shape, its jagged edges and sharp points, and then wander around the Icelandic nature; you'll see Hallgrímskirkja everywhere!

7. ADMIRE THE ARCHITECTURE OF HARPA

A list of tips about Reykjavik would be incomplete without a mention of Harpa and its colorful, enchanting façade. Built as a concert hall and conference center in 2011, Harpa is a stunning example of modern architecture. Its exterior, which – like Hallgrímskirkja –resembles basalt columns, was designed by one of my favorite artists, Ólafur Elíasson. In the morning, the window-covered exterior bathes the building in light, while at night, the windows glow with colorful lights in all hues of the spectrum.

Luckily, Harpa is very conveniently located in downtown Reykjavik, so you can see it both in daylight and at night! Make sure to head inside and roam around the areas that are open to the public, to admire the equally stunning interior architecture.

>TOURIST

8. SEE THE VIEW FROM PERLAN

Perlan (or The Pearl in English) has a strange history. It used to be a water reservoir that provided Reykjavik with hot water, along with its two neighboring reservoirs. However, it is now used as an exhibition center, where you can learn more about Iceland, its volcanoes and its glaciers. There is even a man-made glacial cave right inside, so if you can't visit the real deal, then you have the opportunity to see one up close! Get lost inside the magical tunnels of blue ice, enveloped by the smell of cold and the crackling sounds of the cave's breathing walls.

Then, once you've explored the cave, head up to the top, where you can get a coffee or snack and enjoy a panoramic view of Reykjavik! A 360° deck, wrapped around the top of the building, awaits you to show you the capital from above.

9. VISIT THE POND

The glittering waters of the pond in downtown Reykjavik are a fresh breath of nature in the middle of the city. The pond is surrounded by a small park, which then extends outwards to form a beautiful space for relaxing with a book or taking a walk.

In the winter, the pond's waters freeze. Once the ice is solid enough, dozens of locals grab their ice skates and head to the pond for some family fun!

The pond is also home to swans and ducks all year round, and if, unlike me, you're not deathly afraid of birds, then you can pay them a visit and grab some pictures. They are very friendly!

10. EVERY DAY IS CHRISTMAS AT THE CHRISTMAS STORE

What better place to have a Christmas store that operates throughout the entire year than one of Europe's coldest countries? The OG Christmas store is located in the north of Iceland, in the town of Akureyri. However, if you don't want to go all the way there, you are in luck; there is a Christmas store right in the heart of Reykjavik!

You can find all sorts of goodies there, from Christmas decorations depicting the traditional Icelandic Christmas characters, like the Yule Lads, to Christmas candy and the traditional Icelandic laufabrauð, a disk of thin, fried dough.

Visit the Christmas store to get your Christmas fix even in the middle of the summer!

11. GET A CITY CARD

There is one well-kept secret when it comes to traveling around Reykjavik; the CityCard. Most people traveling to Reykjavik don't even know that this amazing card exists!

For a small amount of money, you can get the CityCard, which grants you free entry to Reykjavik's best museums and galleries, Reykjavik's pools and hot pots, the zoo, and even the buses! It also offers you discounts in several restaurants around Reykjavik, as well as attractions and events.

Make sure to get yourself a CityCard at the start of your trip, to make sure that you don't have to pay an arm and a leg to visit all the best attractions.

12. TIRED OF WALKING? GET AN ELECTRIC SCOOTER

Electric scooters are a new phenomenon in Reykjavik. Many locals like to move around the city on a scooter, since it's environmentally friendly, and they are easily accessible.

Hopp, an electric scooter rental company, has made it easy to get your hands on one. You simply download their app, which finds the nearest scooter for you. Then you scan the scooter's QR code in the app, pay a small fee, and you're on your way!

Because of the tracking system in the scooter, you can leave it anywhere in downtown Reykjavik and the next person will be able to easily locate it! No need to take it back to a specific station!

>TOURIST

WHAT TO DO AND WHAT TO SEE

13. ENJOY A SWIM IN ICELAND'S SWIMMING POOLS

Nothing will make you feel more like a local than soaking in a hot pot in one of Iceland's numerous swimming pools. It is said that there is a pool in every town and village in Iceland, no matter how small, and that some tiny villages don't have high schools, but they do have pools!

Iceland's locals love to spend a calm evening in a hot tub, no matter the weather. In fact, many claim that the best time to go to a hot pot is in the middle of the winter, when the tips of your hair and your eyelashes freeze in the cold, but your body is kept delightfully warm by the water!

Perhaps Icelandic people are enamored by hot tubs because of the strong geothermal activity on the island. They have a long history of soaking in hot water, so much so that the desire is now ingrained in them!

Reykjavik is home to several pools, some of which also boast saunas and steam baths apart from the usual hot pots. They are the perfect place to relax after a day of vigorous sightseeing.

14. RELAX IN A HOT SPRING

Before there were pools and hot pots, there were hot springs. All around Iceland, people have been bathing in hot springs for centuries, the naturally hot waters of lakes and rivers creating the perfect place for a dip.

Due to the intense volcanic activity in Iceland, several underground water channels contain naturally hot water. Once those channels reach the surface, they create a river or lake with hot water.

Some hot springs in Iceland, like the famous Blue Lagoon or its not-so-famous cousin, the Secret Lagoon, charge a fee for entry. The Blue Lagoon, with its milky blue waters, is notoriously expensive, while others, like the Secret Lagoon, are much more affordable. However, there are also several hot springs that you can visit for free! One of the most popular ones is Reykjadalur. After a 45-minute easy hike through the Icelandic nature, you will get to a breathtaking thermal river, which Icelandic people have frequented for centuries. Another free-entry hot spring is the world-famous Seljavallalaug, close to

Seljalandsfoss waterfall, hidden between the mountains in a field of green.

Places like Reykjadalur and Seljavallalaug are the perfect spots to relax in the middle of the praised Icelandic nature, but make sure that you leave nothing but footprints! The free hot springs have no one to keep the area clean or, best case, there are volunteers who clean them, so make sure that you don't leave anything behind.

15. LOOK INTO THE PAST ON A GLACIER

Glaciers and ice caps cover 11% of Iceland, with Vatnajökull being the largest in the country and the second largest in Europe.

There is nothing quite like visiting a glacier. The sheer size of them is enough to make your jaw drop in awe. Once you're on the glacier, you see nothing but white, the vast expanse of ice and snow unfolding in front of you in a reminder that the world might be a small place, but it's also a big one.

Everything is different on such an alien landscape. You can smell the scent of ice, the cold freshness of it. You can hear the wind howl like an ancient, everlasting song in your ears. You can feel the stillness of time, as if the clocks have stopped turning in that piece of land that has been there longer than humans; longer than anything.

Visiting a glacier is an experience like no other, and it comes with a price tag to match. If your budget allows it, though, I would highly recommend it.

16. GET DRENCHED UNDER A WATERFALL

Yet another thing that Iceland has in abundance; waterfalls! It seems like everywhere you look in Iceland, you will find a waterfall, big or small.

The most famous waterfalls in Iceland are Seljalandsfoss and Skógafoss, perhaps partly because of how easy it is to get to them. The former is a beautiful waterfall with a unique structure, as you can walk behind it, while the latter is one of the countrie's biggest waterfalls, and its impressive height of 200 feet sprays so much water that there is almost always a single or double rainbow in front of it!

It would be impossible to list every single waterfall in Iceland under this tip, so I'll give you the names of my favorite ones instead, and leave it up to you to explore the land and find your own favorites. Personally, apart from Seljalandsfoss and Skógafoss, I love Goðafoss, a massive waterfall in northeastern Iceland, and Dynjandi, a group of cascading waterfalls with a collective height of 330 feet!

17. WALK BETWEEN TWO CONTINENTS

We have already seen that there are so many things that make Iceland unique, from glaciers and waterfalls to oases of nature in the middle of the capital. Another thing that is special about Iceland is that it is located on top of the meeting point between two tectonic plates, the Eurasian and the North American.

As the two plates drift apart, the entire island shakes and trembles with the force of strong earthquakes, and the crust bursts open to create volcanoes. At the same time, they make the land expand by about 0.8 inches a year, thus creating a 'walkway' between the two continents! You can find it in Reykjanes, where there is a bridge between the two continents, or in the Thingvellir National Park, where you can walk in the rift or even snorkel in the water that covers part of it!

DAY TRIPS FROM REYKJAVIK

18. VISIT SNÆFELLSNES

Snæfellsnes is perhaps the most underrated area in Iceland, yet it is home to Iceland's most photographed natural landmarks; Kirkjufell. You may recognize its distinct conical shape in pictures, as well as the two waterfalls that flow nearby, making the perfect foreground for a picture of the mountain.

It will take you approximately 12 hours to see the entire peninsula, including Svöðufoss waterfall, a stunning black church, a spring where you can fill your water bottle with natural carbonated water, and of course, Snæfellsnes National Park, with its gorgeous cliffs and beaches.

19. TRAVEL ALONG THE SOUTH SHORE

The South Shore is one of Iceland's most travelled places for a reason. The route follows the southern coast of Iceland, and as you travel, you have the ocean on one side and the cliffs, waterfalls,

>TOURIST

volcanoes, and glaciers on the other! There are so many beautiful sights in the south, and it is one of those trips that you must take when you visit Iceland.

As I mentioned earlier, the South Shore is home to Iceland's two most popular waterfalls, Seljalandsfoss and Skógafoss. However, apart from the waterfalls, there are so many more things to explore!

When you make your way past Seljalandsfoss, look for Seljavallalaug, the hot pool where you can relax for a while before continuing your journey. After Skógafoss, you will come upon a parking lot that is usually packed with cars; that's where another famous Icelandic landmark can be found, usually referred to as simply the plane or the plane crash. There is a hike that will take you approximately an hour (the sign before you begin your walk will inform you that it will take you four hours one way, but I have been there multiple times and I can assure you that if you are relatively healthy and fit, it won't take you over an hour), where you will walk in a vast black sand beach with seemingly no end in sight in any direction, a piece of land that looks like it jumped straight out of a Hollywood movie about an alien planet. The hike itself is enjoyable, with the desert of black sand creating the perfect backdrop for your short journey. Eventually, you will get to an abandoned United States Navy DC plane that crash-landed on the beach in 1973 after running out of fuel. Not to worry! The pilot was fine and walked the same path you will be taking until he found a nearby village.

The plane makes for the perfect subject for a photograph and the black sand the perfect backdrop. If you walk a little further down, you will get to the ocean, where the foamy white waves meet the black pebbles of the beach.

Then, you can continue your journey towards Dyrhólaey. The cliffs tower over the ocean, and in the summer, they are the perfect place to spot and photograph some puffins! After Dyrhólaey, make your way to Reynisfjara, or as it is more commonly known in English, the Black Sand Beach. There are plenty of black sand beaches in Iceland; in fact most beaches here are covered in black sand, and the white sand that covers most European and American coastlines is very rare. What makes Reynisfjara special, though, are the basalt columns covering the side of the beach, as well as two rock formations in the sea. Legend has it that the rocks were trolls, who turned to stone after not making it back to their cave in the mountains in time to avoid the sun.

At this time, you can head back to Reykjavik and conclude your day trip. However, if you have time or if you would like to camp for the night, you can continue on eastwards to see the Glacier Lagoon. There you can see a lake full of icebergs that float on the waters, cracking and breaking under their own

>TOURIST

weight, sinking and reappearing at the surface; everchanging. The charm of the Glacier Lagoon is that it's never the same, changing within seconds.

20. VISIT THE GOLDEN CIRCLE

The Golden Circle is the quickest day trip you can take in Iceland, taking about eight hours with stops to complete. There are two ways to do this trip; either start from Thingvellir and go clockwise or start from Geysir and go counterclockwise. Personally, I prefer the second way, as there is a hidden place that I love to visit before I begin the trip, called Friðheimar. Friðheimar is a tomato farm that is focused on everything tomato. You can get a hearty bowl of tomato soup, as well tomato jam and even tomato beer!

Once you've satisfied your tomato cravings, head to Geysir, Iceland's most famous geyser. There, you can see water explode out of the ground every two to eight minutes, in what I like to think as nature's fireworks. The geyser never fails to delight me!

Fun fact: the geyser you will see errupting is, in fact, Strokkur, Geysir's little brother. Geysir stopped errupting a few decades ago, but thankfully we still have Strokkur!

After Geysir, head to Gullfoss, which translates to the Golden Waterfall in English. Gullfoss is truly a spectacular sight, with its waters rushing down with incredible force. You can see it from the top to get a panoramic view, but you can also head down and see it up close, if you don't mind getting drenched!

Lastly, you will head to Thingvellir National Park, one of my favorite places in Iceland. As I mentioned earlier, there you can walk between the tectonic plates, as well as go snorkelling in the crystal-clear waters of Silfra, a part of the tectonic rift. There are also several other sights to explore, including a lake and my favorite small waterfall, Öxarárfoss.

The Golden Circle truly deserves its name, and you will find that it's a trip impossible to forget.

21. VISIT REYKJANES

Reykjanes is another underrated area in Iceland, especially since it's so easily accessible. It's the peninsula where the airport is located, only forty minutes from Reykjavik, but even so, it's not very popular with tourists, despite its undeniable beauty.

>TOURIST

Reykjanes is a geothermal area, and therefore there is a lot of interesting, almost alien landscapes to explore. Gunnuhver is perhaps the most popular one, an area with intense geothermal activity, where steam constantly comes out of the ground. The boiling water has carved the earth into little mud pools that bubble continuously, and the steam meets the clouds as it drifts up into the sky.

You can also find Brimketill in Reykjanes, a small lava pool that has been naturally carved into the sea, as well as Kleifarvatn, a hilly area with beautiful expansions of black sand beaches.

Since it's so close to the airport and the Blue Lagoon, you can explore Reykjanes when you arrive or when you visit the lagoon.

22. HIKE UP ESJA

When the locals of Reykjavik want to take a break from their busy city life or enjoy a rare sunny day, there is one place that we go; Esja. Esja is a mountain just outside Reykjavik, and it's a popular hiking spot for locals who want to spend a few hours in nature.

Esja has three hiking trails with varying difficulties, so almost everyone can go to the top! Your hike is perfectly complemented by the trees and rivers that surround the paths, and you will meet a lot of locals on the way. Feel free to talk to them! Icelandic people love to chat and talk about their country!

23. HIKE AND SOAK IN REYKJADALUR

Can't get enough of hiking? Then Reykjadalur is for you.

Personally, I prefer Reykjadalur over Esja, even though it is forty minutes from Reykjavik, as I am not a big fan of hiking. Therefore, I like that Reykjadalur has a reward at the end; a breathtaking valley with a thermal river running through it, where you can sit and relax!

The river has varying temperatures, as the further up you go, the hotter it gets. So, you can find the spot with the perfect temperature for you! The hike to the river takes less than an hour, approximately 45 minutes, and then you are free to soak in the thermal waters for as long as you like.

In the summer, you will also find sheep in the area, as Icelandic sheep are free to roam during the summer months! Nothing beats Reykjadalur's view, with the green valley and the grazing sheep!

GETTING AROUND

24. RENT A CAR

If you want to explore Iceland at your own pace and discover places where most tourists don't go, then your best bet is renting a car. Renting a car in Iceland can be very expensive, especially if you are planning on visiting the highlands, where you will need a specific kind of 4x4. However, if it is within your budget, then it's the best way to travel around the country.

There are several companies you can choose, and all of them are in the same price range, with the same policies. It's hard to go wrong on that one. However, when traveling by car in Iceland, be very careful. Often, even in the summer in certain places, road conditions are dangerous. Icelandic roads outside of Reykjavik are full of twists and turns, dangerous hills, one-lane bridges, and dirt roads. It's easy to get in an accident if you aren't careful.

Furthermore, be aware of police and cameras, as the fines for going over the speed limit are steep. Trust me, you do not want to pay them.

Other than that, make sure to enjoy the beautiful drive! Even from a car, the Icelandic nature is a sight to behold.

25. BOOK A TOUR

If you don't feel like driving, there are several tours you can take to explore the country. Every travel company offers tours to the most popular destinations, including the South Shore, the Golden Circle, and Snæfellsnes.

Do your research and pick the company that fits you best. Some companies only offer big group tours, while others offer tours for smaller groups, for a more personal and enjoyable experience. There are also several offers and discounts, as well as partnerships between companies that will help you save a pretty penny.

>TOURIST

26. TAKE THE BUS

I wouldn't recommend the bus if you are planning to go outside of Reykjavik. There are some routes you can take that will take you, for example, to Reykjadalur, but it will take much longer than driving yourself or taking a tour.

If you are traveling within Reykjavik, though, the bus is a great way to explore the city. As with every bus system, the Icelandic bus system has its problems, with occasional delays and packed buses, at least downtown. However, when the weather is too bad to walk or when you need to get a little further than where your feet can take you, the bus is the perfect way to travel.

ICELANDIC DELIGHTS

27. EAT THE WORLD'S BEST HOT DOG

It must seem odd that I am beginning this section of the tips with the hot dog; the humble, unassuming hot dog. When you get to Iceland, though, you will soon find that Icelandic people love their hot dogs almost as much as they love their pools.

You can find hot dogs virtually everywhere, from gas stations to food stands. Bæjarins Beztu Pylsur, or The Best Hot Dog In Town in English, is –as its name suggests –often hailed as the best hot dog stand in Reykjavik. It's conveniently located in downtown Reykjavik, in Tryggvagata, but you will often find a colossal queue of people waiting in line for their hot dog.

Besides, it's not even the best hot dog in my opinion. If you want the opinion of a local, I suggest that you get it from the stand in Selfoss, at least if you find yourself going that way. Their toasted bun is the perfect crunchy companion to the delicious dog.

28. INDULGE IN CANDY (OR AS WE SAY, NAMMI)

Candy is a big part of Iceland's culture. Every supermarket and corner shop has a section of pick'n'mix, where you can get your nammi fix.

No one really knows where that love of candy originated, but everyone seems glad that it exists. Candy can be very expensive, though, so indulge in pick'n'mix on the weekends, when most stores have a discount, or buy packaged candy. My favorites? Thristur, Nóa Kropp, and Hraun.

29. GIVE THE DRIED FISH A TRY

You might be surprised to know that before WWII, Iceland was a very poor country, one of the poorest in the world. Therefore, people needed to keep their food stored somehow, so they could make it last for a long time.

Enter the dried fish. It is exactly what it sounds like; a fish that has been left out to dry. If it sounds disgusting, well . . . that's because it kind of is. Dried fish seems to be an acquired taste, and while Icelandic people love it and swear by its health benefits (dried fish is a great source of protein), people who didn't grow up eating it don't seem to like it.

Don't let that scare you, though! Give it a try and find out for yourself!

30. A TASTE FOX A DAY WILL MAKE YOU WANT TO STAY

What is a taste fox, I imagine you ask. Taste fox is the straight translation of bragðarefur, and the crazy cousin of the McFlurry. It's a copious amount of vanilla ice cream (even the small sizes are as big as my head), mixed with your choice of usually three different types of candy or fruit.

Sounds like a dream? I can assure you it's real; and it's perhaps the best thing you can eat in Iceland!

31. TASTE TRADITION WITH LAMB AND LAMB SOUP

When looking for traditional Icelandic food, lamb soup is the best there is.

Lamb is quite a strange meat; I personally hate the taste and smell of lamb, and everyone I know in Iceland insists that Icelandic lamb is different than any other lamb in the world, and that I should like it.

I don't. But I also don't necessarily hate it. I've had lamb soup in Iceland that is perfectly savory and delicious, making the smell of the meat bearable. And, well, if you like lamb, then you will love Icelandic lamb!

32. TRY THE WORLD-FAMOUS SKYR

You may have seen skyr around in the fancier supermarkets in other countries, marketed as a superfood that is packed with protein.

In Iceland, people knew about the benefits of skyr for decades. While it has the consistency of Greek yogurt, skyr is technically cheese. Think of it more as a yogurt, though, because it is smooth and a little sweet and tangy, and even yummier with flavors like chocolate or coconut.

You will find skyr virtually anywhere in Iceland, from its humble, packaged form in the supermarkets to being part of fancy desserts in fine dining establishments.

However you like to eat your skyr, plain or flavored, it makes for the perfect breakfast to start your day with energy!

33. TRY BRENNIVÍN ... IF YOU DARE

You may have heard of Brennivín already. This alcoholic drink is found everywhere in Iceland, though it's very hard to find abroad, and its 40% alcoholic content is guaranteed to make you have a great time.

Brennivín is also referred to as Black Death, but the literal translation to English would be 'burning wine'. Though it is considered a traditional liquor, it was in fact introduced in 1935, when the alcohol prohibition ended in Iceland.

Brennivín is made of fermented grain or potato mash, and it is flavored with carraway, which gives it its distinct flavor. Traditionally, you can enjoy Brennivín with hákarl, which is a type of rotten shark (yes, that's a thing people used to it in Iceland). Feel free to skip the shark, though! Brennivín tastes just as good – if not better –on its own!

>TOURIST

SOUVENIRS TO REMIND YOU OF YOUR TRAVELS

34. LOPAPEYSA KNITTED BY A GRANDMA

When you think about Icelandic people, do you imagine them in those wool sweaters with the cute patterns? You're not too far off.

While you won't see Icelanders dress in a wool sweater (or lopapeysa) every day, it is still a staple of their wardrobe, and it's the best souvenir you can buy.

Icelandic wool sweaters are made from lopi, a kind of wool that is unspun and that comes from Icelandic sheep. As the yarn is not spun, it contains more air than spun yarn, and that means that it will keep you warmer on those chilly Icelandic days!

Every Icelandic person has at least a couple lopapeysur knitted by their grandma. But you're not an Icelander, so what can you do to get your hands on one? Well, there are several stores that cater to your needs, but the prices are steep and, let's face it, they are not really traditional, as they were made by a machine. There are several secondhand stores in

Reykjavik where you can get an authentic lopapeysa knitted by a grandma, and that will cost you less than a new one from a store. However, if you want the ultimate Icelandic experience, then there are several groups and people on Facebook that you can contact ahead of your trip, and they will knit a lopapeysa just for you!

If you do get one, make sure you treat it with care. Wool is a delicate fabric, and in order to wash it, you will need cold water and a gentle detergent. Unless it's really dirty, though, you don't even need to wash it! The great thing about a lopapeysa is that you can leave it hanging in the wind, and the wind will clear all the dirt and debris out, as the wool fibers that make up the yarn are very smooth and dirt doesn't cling onto them!

35. TAKE A TASTE OF ICELAND HOME WITH YOU WITH SOME CANDY

For a very affordable and mouthwatering souvenir, take some candy home with you! After all, candy is so important to the Icelandic culture, and there are so many different varieties to choose from! Stock up on your favorite candy until your next trip to Iceland, and you'll feel like you never left!

36. INDULGE IN HANDMADE JEWELRY

Lately, several different boutiques have opened in Reykjavik, both as physical stores and online. Their specialty? Handmade jewelry.

Reykjavik is famous for its art and design, and it seems like the city's artists are now focusing their efforts and talents on creating gorgeous jewelry with Reykjavik's signature Nordic design. If you like simple, stackable rings, elegant earrings, and delicate necklaces, then you will love Icelandic jewelry!

The artists use primarily sterling silver, and often coat it in gold or rose gold. Common stones that you can find include pyrite, pearls, and Herkimer diamonds, and sometimes even lava stones, though it's almost impossible to find jewelry with real Icelandic lava stones, as it's very hard to work with them.

The jewelry is often very affordable, and can be worn every day as a reminder of your trip!

WHAT FESTIVALS TO ATTEND

37. PARTY LIKE A LOCAL AT ÞJÓÐHÁTÍÐ

If there is one thing that Icelandic people crave for throughout the year, that's Þjóðhátíð (Thjóðhátíð). The annual festival is held on the weekend before the first Monday of August, and the locals flock to the Westman Islands in the thousands for three days of non-stop fun and music.

Attendees typically camp near the volcanic crater where the concert is held (the naturally round shape of the crater creates the perfect acoustics) for the duration of the festival. The acts are Icelandic, and while you wouldn't understand the lyrics, you also probably wouldn't care. After all, you don't go to Þjóðhátíð for the music; you go for the atmosphere.

Þjóðhátíð is also a great opportunity to explore the largest of the Westman Islands, Heimaey, a beautiful place with a rich history.

38. ENJOY MUSIC UNDER THE MIDNIGHT SUN AT SECRET SOLSTICE

Secret Solstice is like Þjóðhátíð but for Reykjavik. It takes place right in the heart of the capital, on the weekend of the summer solstice, which means that you will party under the sun the entire day and night!

Secret Solstice hosts both foreign and local acts, as well as some big names every year. If you want to get a taste of the Icelandic music scene without leaving Reykjavik, then this one's for you!

39. SEE UNDERGROUND ACTS IN REYKJAVIK'S BEST VENUES AT ICELAND AIRWAVES

Iceland Airwaves is a little different from the other two festivals. For starters, it takes place in November. That might sound strange for a music festival, but the venues are all indoors, so don't worry that you'll be drenched in rain!

The festival hosts mainly alternative acts, and utilizes Reykjavik's strangest venues, including hostels, bars, and churches! There is something in practically every corner of Reykjavik for you to enjoy!

40. TRY MOUTHWATERING DELICACIES AT REYKJAVIK FOOD FESTIVAL

If you're not much of a concert person, but more of a foodie, then I have the perfect festival for you. The Reykjavik Food Festival takes place in August, and it's the best place to try some Icelandic cuisine.

Reykjavik's best chefs gather to make traditional and modern Icelandic dishes, and you are bound to leave the festival with a full belly and a smile!

>TOURIST

ACTIVITIES FOR THE WHOLE FAMILY

41. GO SKIING

Skiing is a favorite activity among Icelandic people. If you visit in the winter and want to spend a day like a real local, then skiing is the best thing you can do!

There are plenty of ski resorts around Iceland, the most renowned being the one in Akureyri. With a number of different slopes for all levels of experience, the ski resort in the capital of the north is the best place to spend a day full of fun! Make sure to head to the local swimming pool afterwards, which is often hailed as the best swimming pool in Iceland, for a relaxing soak to rest your muscles!

If you can't go all the way to Akureyri to ski, then Bláfjöll (the Blue Mountain) is the place for you. This ski resort is only about half an hour's drive from Reykjavik, making it very convenient for you to pop by and ski to your heart's desire!

Every ski resort in Iceland has, of course, rentals for skiing and safety equipment, as well as cafeterias where you can take a break and have a snack.

42. TRY SNOWMOBILING

Out of all the activities I have tried in Iceland (and trust me, I have tried many!), the best, most exciting, and most unforgettable one is by far snowmobiling.

Most tour companies will take you on a trip to Langjökull ice cap for a snowmobile ride, and as Langjökull is very close to the Golden Circle, you can combine it with a tour of the area!

Langjökull takes its name from its shape, which makes it the longest ice cap in the country, measuring at 31 miles long. Once you get to the ice cap, you will feel just how massive it is, the whiteness of the ice stretching ahead of you seemingly endlessly. The horizon meets the ground, and it's hard to tell where the land stops and the sky begins, the entire world blending into a shade of pure white.

As you can't access the glaciers and ice caps with a regular car, a modified bus (with tires as big as an adult of average height) will take you to the hut where you will prepare for your trip. There, you will get the necessary equipment, and then you will get your snowmobile and instructions, and off you'll go!

Make sure to always follow your guide, as ice caps and glaciers can be treacherous. Your guide will know where the ice is thin and will avoid those spots, so that you can have a safe and fun experience.

43. GO ON A GLACIER HIKE

If you're not one for speed, you can go on a glacier hike instead. Walking on a glacier is unlike anything you have experienced before. There are miles separating you from the nearest point where the ground isn't covered by ice, and you walk on the white and blue, trekking up some of the world's most hostile, yet calming environments.

Once again, you must always have a guide when you go glacier hiking, as there are rifts in the ice that you have to avoid. Several tour companies offer glacier hikes as an option, and they will provide you with the necessary equipment you'll need. Some tours even teach you to climb on the ice if you want to!

At the end of your hike, you might be lucky enough to find an ice cave and see the glacier from the inside. The walls of ice caves are always so blue when the light hits them, like pieces of aquamarine.

44. SIGHTSEE AT THE SEA

Who doesn't love an adorable critter? Iceland is home to several different animals, including different species of whales, as well as seals and tortoises. The best way to see them is by taking a whale watching tour!

There is a huge number of whale watching tours available in Iceland, and some of them leave right from the heart of Reykjavik! The ocean around Reykjavik is full of ocean creatures, and you can often see playful whales swim around the ships.

However, the best place to see whales is without a doubt Húsavík, a town in the north. The waters near Húsavík are the perfect environment for whales and seals to thrive, and it's unlikely that you won't catch a glimpse of them playing around in the waters.

>TOURIST

45. TRY TO SEE SOME PUFFINS

Puffins are often hailed as the most adorable animals in Iceland. A bird that only calls Iceland home for a couple of months in the summertime, puffins have been an Icelandic delicacy for a long time.

You're not here to eat them, though; you're here to see them. Puffins are notoriously elusive, but they are not really afraid of humans, so it's easy to spot them if you're at the right place at the right time. As with whale watching, there are plenty of puffin watching tours in Iceland that you can do by boat, and the best ones leave from Reykjavik, so it's easy to catch one of them.

If you are dying to see some puffins, then there are two spots for you where you will have the best chance to spot them in the mainland: Dyrhólaey in the south shore, and the Látrabjarg cliffs in the Westfjords.

46. RIDE THE WORLD-FAMOUS ICELANDIC HORSE

Yet another thing that Iceland is famous for around the world; the Icelandic horse!

The Icelandic horse is a breed that is unique to Iceland, though it is genetically related to the Mongolian horse. It is believed that the Mongolian horse came to Sweden through Russia by Swedish traders, and eventually, between 860 and 935 AD, the ancestors of the Icelandic horse were brought to Iceland by the Vikings.

The modern-day Icelandic horse is the result of selective breeding. It's small in size, but it's very strong, and what it lacks in height, it makes up for in temperament and talent. The Icelandic horse is, in fact, the only horse in the world that has five gaits! One of its gaits is renowned for the comfort with which it provides the rider, as it's very smooth and the rider seems to barely move while on horseback.

Therefore, it's needless to say that riding an Icelandic horse is one of the most fun activities you can do in Iceland! A bonus? They love to be pet!

47. ACHING FOR SOME OFF-ROADING? GO ON AN ATV RIDE

I mentioned early in this guide that you should never go off-roading in Iceland, especially not over moss-covered lava fields. If you are itching for some off-roading action, there is a way to get your fix!

Enter the ATV. ATV rides are quite popular in Iceland, especially with tourists. There is just something so fun about taking a vehicle off the road and driving around in uneven, rough terrain!

Many tour companies offer ATV tours, and though they are rather expensive, they are worth every penny. Your tour guide will take you to places where off-roading is legal and won't damage the fragile Icelandic nature, and you can take your ATV for a spin without worrying about your impact on the land or getting fined. Besides, since you will be in an ATV, there is no risk of damaging the vehicle, so you can have all the fun in the world!

WHAT TO PACK FOR YOUR TRIP

48. FOR THE WINTER

The most common question from travelers is what they should pack when they come to Iceland. As someone who has lived here long enough to know how the seasons can change within a day, I can tell you that you will need a number of different things for your stay in the country.

In the winter, you will need to stay warm, but also be able to remove clothing when you are indoors. Therefore, you should wear at least three layers at all times, not including your jacket. Thermals are always a good option, as are fabrics like wool, and moisture-wicking base layers.

You should also have warm socks, a beanie, and gloves, as well as a raincoat for when you visit the waterfalls. You definitely don't want to be wet for the rest of the day or you'll catch a cold!

Furthermore, make sure you have a good jacket. If you come from a warm country and don't own a good winter jacket, preferably a down one, then you can rent a jacket from a clothing store called Cintamani. Buying a winter jacket in Iceland will set you back hundreds of dollars, so renting one for the duration of your trip is a much more affordable option.

Finally, don't forget your swimsuit! Yes, I know we are talking about winter, but even in the winter you will want to visit the pools and hot springs, so a swimsuit is a must!

49. FOR THE SUMMER

Summers in Iceland are often a time of confusion and despair. Don't get me wrong, I love summers and I love Iceland; I just never know what to wear!

They say that in Iceland, if you don't like the weather, wait five seconds. That is especially true in the summer, when it can be sunny and warm one minute, and raining the next. You never know what you're going to get in the summer months, so it's better to be prepared.

Once again, make sure you pack a swimsuit, as you will be needing it a lot! You might also need t-shirts and shorts for those days when the sun is shining and there is no cloud in sight.

On top of that, you will also need some layers, such as sweaters and cardigans, as well as the must-have raincoat for visiting the waterfalls.

50. DON'T FORGET YOUR CAMERA

If there is one thing that you absolutely have to have with you, that is a camera! Not only will you want to take pictures to remember your trip, but the landscapes and the nature of Iceland are so stunning that you will definitely want to capture them in a picture forever!

There are so many things to see, explore, and photograph, and you will leave the country with a camera full of memories.

>TOURIST

CAN'T GET ENOUGH? HERE ARE SOME BONUS TIPS

1. CAPTURE THE NORTHERN LIGHTS

I'm sure you were wondering when I would come to this tip.

After all, the northern lights are one of Iceland's most famous attractions! That's why I thought this tip would be better suited to this Bonus Tips list!

In order to capture the northern lights, you need a proper camera and a tripod. A phone camera will just not cut it most of the time, and you will need to do a long exposure, so you need a tripod or at least something where you can prop your camera up.

Make sure to bundle up before you leave your hotel room, as the northern lights are quite capricious, and it will take you a while to find them. Then, head out to an area without any light pollution. There are several places around Reykjavik that have no street lights, and they are perfect for seeing the northern lights, but the further you can go from the city, the better your chances.

Once you find the perfect spot, set up your tripod and put your camera to its widest aperture. Make sure you are zoomed all the way out, set your ISO to around 800, turn off image stabilization, set a two-second timer, and do a long exposure (5 to 10 seconds is usually the best to capture the lights without having too much motion in the stars). Voila, you have a beautiful picture of the northern lights!

Travel companies also offer northern lights tours, and they will take you to the best spots where you can see them. Remember, though, that there is no guarantee the lights will be visible on any day, so you have to hunt and hope!

Also remember that the northern lights are only visible in the dark, so you can only see them in the winter months, as it doesn't get dark in the summer! In order to see the northern lights, you should visit Iceland from around the end of August to the end of March, though the best times are from October to February.

2. ENJOY THE MIDNIGHT SUN

The midnight sun is, naturally, much easier to enjoy than the northern lights. Throughout the summer months, and especially around the summer solstice, the sun never sets in Iceland! That is because the country is so far up north that it faces the sun constantly due to Earth's tilt.

It can be rather disorienting at first to wake up and go to sleep with the sun shining bright in the sky, but that is why Icelanders have black-out curtains in their bedrooms (and hotels). Despite how strange it might seem, the midnight sun is bound to give you endless energy all day, so you will find it very easy to explore the country for hours! Just make sure to check your clock every now and then, as the constant light can mess up your circadian rhythms and make you forget to eat!

3. DRINKING ALCOHOL? GET IT AT THE DUTY FREE

If there is one tip that every Icelandic person would give you,

that would be to shop at the duty free for alcohol when you arrive in Iceland.

Alcohol in Iceland is insanely expensive, so much so that even Icelandic people only shop their alcohol in the country only if they have no choice. They tend to shop their own alcohol at the duty free when they return home from trips overseas, and stock up for when they need it.

The reason for the sky-high prices is that the government taxes liquor like no other product, and every liquor store is owned by the government.

Liquor stores are also closed on Sundays, as well as every day after five in the afternoon, so it can also be hard to get alcohol. So, save yourself form the expensive bottles of liquor and stock up when you are at the airport.

4. GO GROCERY SHOPPING TO STAY WITHIN BUDGET

You may have realized by now that everything in Iceland is very expensive. Import taxes and shipping fees are charged on the customers, after all, and so you can easily go over your budget while traveling around Iceland.

One way to avoid that is by eating out during lunch hours, when most restaurants have lunch offers, and getting the rest of your food from grocery stores.

The cheapest grocery store chain, and the most popular one, is Bónus, and they have several locations around the Capital Region, including Reykjavik. It's the best place to stock up on some food and toiletries, so look for one of them while traveling. Like Bonus, Krónan is also a budget supermarket with several locations in Reykjavik.

Another option is Nettó, which is a little pricier, but is open all day, every day. If you need something in a pinch, it's the best place to find it, even in the middle of the night.

The one store you should avoid at all costs is 10/11. This chain has locations all around downtown Reykjavik, but you will rarely, if ever, see a local there. Why? Well, they are ridiculously overpriced, and even the most common items will cost you an arm and a leg. There is no reason to shop there when you have so many other options that will charge you a much fairer price!

\>TOURIST

TOP REASONS TO BOOK THIS TRIP

Nature: The Icelandic nature is one of the best in the whole world. The black sand beaches that stretch as far as the eye can see, the eternal pure white ice caps, the moss-covered lava fields, and the geothermal areas covered in steam make for an alien landscape that you can't find anywhere else.

Adventure: Iceland's unique nature is also the perfect place for some adventure! You can walk behind waterfalls, ski on steep slopes, snowmobile on ice caps, and even climb on ice! What better way to satisfy your desire for adventure?

Relaxation: While Iceland can offer you plenty of opportunities for adventure, it can also offer you the most relaxing places and activities in the world. You can relax in its naturally warm waters, soak in its pools, and sweat your stress away in its steam baths!

>TOURIST

OTHER RESOURCES:

City Card: https://visitreykjavik.is/city-card/front

Electric scooters: https://hopp.bike/

Buses of Reykjavik and route planner: https://www.straeto.is/en

Wake Up Reykjavik blog: https://wakeupreykjavik.com/things-to-do-in-iceland/

Secret Solstice: https://secretsolstice.is/

Iceland Airwaves: https://icelandairwaves.is/

Best places to see the northern lights in Iceland map: https://www.google.is/maps/@64.9261764,-22.3027728,7z/data=!3m1!4b1!4m2!6m

1!1s1VuaibUGVbkHqBnCpwxzOa8z8TnMkQRw0?hl=en&authuser=0

Best things to see in the Snæfellsnes peninsula map: https://www.google.is/maps/@64.8447424,-23.1991376,9z/data=!3m1!4b1!4m2!6m1!1s16YnrdJLw6l6L7BWi7JPfd-N-2zz8b5za?hl=en&authuser=0

Best things to see in the South Shore map: https://www.google.is/maps/@63.7271279,-20.4987028,8z/data=!3m1!4b1!4m2!6m1!1s1BDSblGr88x6EWk4dNlmj8xlq2xq_xTud?hl=en&authuser=0

Best things to see in the Golden Circle map: https://www.google.is/maps/@64.2521501,-20.8253249,10z/data=!3m1!4b1!4m2!6m1!1s1SW753ZtWbuBxHls3qSJYlPlvjPPho895?hl=en&authuser=0

>TOURIST

PACKING AND PLANNING TIPS

A Week before Leaving

- Arrange for someone to take care of pets and water plants.
- Email and Print important Documents.
- Get Visa and vaccines if needed.
- Check for travel warnings.
- Stop mail and newspaper.
- Notify Credit Card companies where you are going.
- Passports and photo identification is up to date.
- Pay bills.
- Copy important items and download travel Apps.
- Start collecting small bills for tips.
- Have post office hold mail while you are away.
- Check weather for the week.
- Car inspected, oil is changed, and tires have the correct pressure.
- Check airline luggage restrictions.
- Download Apps needed for your trip.

Right Before Leaving

- Contact bank and credit cards to tell them your location.
- Clean out refrigerator.
- Empty garbage cans.
- Lock windows.
- Make sure you have the proper identification with you.
- Bring cash for tips.
- Remember travel documents.
- Lock door behind you.
- Remember wallet.
- Unplug items in house and pack chargers.
- Change your thermostat settings.
- Charge electronics, and prepare camera memory cards.

>TOURIST

READ OTHER GREATER THAN A TOURIST BOOKS

Greater Than a Tourist- Geneva Switzerland: 50 Travel Tips from a Local by Amalia Kartika

Greater Than a Tourist- St. Croix US Birgin Islands USA: 50 Travel Tips from a Local by Tracy Birdsall

Greater Than a Tourist- San Juan Puerto Rico: 50 Travel Tips from a Local by Melissa Tait

Greater Than a Tourist – Lake George Area New York USA: 50 Travel Tips from a Local by Janine Hirschklau

Greater Than a Tourist – Monterey California United States: 50 Travel Tips from a Local by Katie Begley

Greater Than a Tourist – Cnanai Crete Greece: 50 Travel Tips from a Local by Dimitra Papagrigoraki

Greater Than a Tourist – The Garden Route Western Cape Province South Africa: 50 Travel Tips from a Local by Li-Anne McGregor van Aardt

Greater Than a Tourist – Sevilla Andalusia Spain: 50 Travel Tips from a Local by Gabi Gazon

Children's Book: *Charlie the Cavalier Travels the World* by Lisa Rusczyk Ed. D.

> TOURIST

Follow us on Instagram for beautiful travel images:
http://Instagram.com/GreaterThanATourist

Follow *Greater Than a Tourist* on Amazon.
>Tourist Podcast
>T Website
>T Youtube
>T Facebook
>T TikTok
>T Goodreads
>T Amazon
>T Mailing List
>T Pinterest
>T Instagram
>T Twitter
>T SoundCloud
>T LinkedIn
>T Map

> TOURIST

At *Greater Than a Tourist*, we love to share travel tips with you. How did we do? What guidance do you have for how we can give you better advice for your next trip? Please send your feedback to GreaterThanaTourist@gmail.com as we continue to improve the series. We appreciate your constructive feedback. Thank you.

>TOURIST

METRIC CONVERSIONS

TEMPERATURE

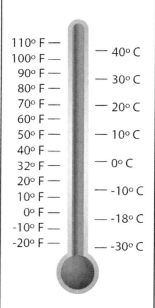

110° F	— 40° C
100° F	
90° F	— 30° C
80° F	
70° F	— 20° C
60° F	
50° F	— 10° C
40° F	
32° F	— 0° C
20° F	
10° F	— -10° C
0° F	
-10° F	— -18° C
-20° F	— -30° C

To convert F to C:
Subtract 32, and then multiply by 5/9 or .5555.

To Convert C to F:
Multiply by 1.8 and then add 32.

32F = 0C

LIQUID VOLUME

To Convert:.................Multiply by
U.S. Gallons to Liters................. 3.8
U.S. Liters to Gallons 26
Imperial Gallons to U.S. Gallons 1.2
Imperial Gallons to Liters....... 4.55
Liters to Imperial Gallons 22
1 Liter = .26 U.S. Gallon
1 U.S. Gallon = 3.8 Liters

DISTANCE

To convert ....Multiply by
Inches to Centimeters 2.54
Centimeters to Inches 39
Feet to Meters........................3
Meters to Feet 3.28
Yards to Meters 91
Meters to Yards 1.09
Miles to Kilometers 1.61
Kilometers to Miles............ .62
1 Mile = 1.6 km
1 km = .62 Miles

WEIGHT

1 Ounce = .28 Grams
1 Pound = .4555 Kilograms
1 Gram = .04 Ounce
1 Kilogram = 2.2 Pounds

>TOURIST

TRAVEL QUESTIONS

- Do you bring presents home to family or friends after a vacation?
- Do you get motion sick?
- Do you have a favorite billboard?
- Do you know what to do if there is a flat tire?
- Do you like a sun roof open?
- Do you like to eat in the car?
- Do you like to wear sun glasses in the car?
- Do you like toppings on your ice cream?
- Do you use public bathrooms?
- Did you bring a cell phone and does it have power?
- Do you have a form of identification with you?
- Have you ever been pulled over by a cop?
- Have you ever given money to a stranger on a road trip?
- Have you ever taken a road trip with animals?
- Have you ever gone on a vacation alone?
- Have you ever run out of gas?

- If you could move to any place in the world, where would it be?
- If you could travel anywhere in the world, where would you travel?
- If you could travel in any vehicle, which one would it be?
- If you had three things to wish for from a magic genie, what would they be?
- If you have a driver's license, how many times did it take you to pass the test?
- What are you the most afraid of on vacation?
- What do you want to get away from the most when you are on vacation?
- What foods smell bad to you?
- What item do you bring on ever trip with you away from home?
- What makes you sleepy?
- What song would you love to hear on the radio when you're cruising on the highway?
- What travel job would you want the least?
- What will you miss most while you are away from home?
- What is something you always wanted to try?

>TOURIST

- What is the best road side attraction that you ever saw?
- What is the farthest distance you ever biked?
- What is the farthest distance you ever walked?
- What is the weirdest thing you needed to buy while on vacation?
- What is your favorite candy?
- What is your favorite color car?
- What is your favorite family vacation?
- What is your favorite food?
- What is your favorite gas station drink or food?
- What is your favorite license plate design?
- What is your favorite restaurant?
- What is your favorite smell?
- What is your favorite song?
- What is your favorite sound that nature makes?
- What is your favorite thing to bring home from a vacation?
- What is your favorite vacation with friends?
- What is your favorite way to relax?

- Where is the farthest place you ever traveled in a car?
- Where is the farthest place you ever went North, South, East and West?
- Where is your favorite place in the world?
- Who is your favorite singer?
- Who taught you how to drive?
- Who will you miss the most while you are away?
- Who if the first person you will contact when you get to your destination?
- Who brought you on your first vacation?
- Who likes to travel the most in your life?
- Would you rather be hot or cold?
- Would you rather drive above, below, or at the speed limited?
- Would you rather drive on a highway or a back road?
- Would you rather go on a train or a boat?
- Would you rather go to the beach or the woods?

>TOURIST

TRAVEL BUCKET LIST

1.

2.

3.

4.

5.

6.

7.

8.

9.

10.

>TOURIST

NOTES

Made in United States
North Haven, CT
09 April 2022